Basketball's MVPs

Dan Osier

TIM DUNCAN

PowerKiDS
press

New York

Published in 2011 by The Rosen Publishing Group, Inc.
29 East 21st Street, New York, NY 10010

Copyright © 2011 by The Rosen Publishing Group, Inc.

First Edition

Editor: Amelie von Zumbusch
Book Design: Kate Laczynski

Photo Credits: Cover, p. 1 Chris Graythen/Getty Images; pp. 4, 22 Ronald Martinez/Getty Images; pp. 6—7 D. Clarke Evans/ NBAE/Getty Images; p. 8 Ezra Shaw/Getty Images; p. 11 Doug Pensinger/Getty Images; p. 12 Todd Warshaw/Getty Images; p. 14—15 Andrew B. Bernstein/NBAE/Getty Images; p. 16 Paul Buck/ AFP/Getty Images; pp. 18—19 Greg Nelson/Sports Illustrated/ Getty Images; p. 20 Chris Ivey/NBAE/Getty Images.

Library of Congress Cataloging-in-Publication Data

Osier, Dan.
 Tim Duncan / by Dan Osier. — 1st ed.
   p. cm. — (Basketball's MVPs)
 Includes index.
 ISBN 978-1-4488-2527-1 (library binding) —
 ISBN 978-1-4488-2638-4 (pbk.) — ISBN 978-1-4488-2639-1
 (6-pack)
 1. Duncan, Tim, 1976– 2. Basketball players—United States—
Biography. 3. San Antonio Spurs (Basketball team) I. Title.
 GV884.D86O753 2011
 796.323092—dc22
 [B]
                    2010028003

Manufactured in the United States of America

CPSIA Compliance Information: Batch #WW11PK: For Further Information contact Rosen Publishing, New York, New York at 1-800-237-9932

CONTENTS

Tim Duncan plays basketball for the San Antonio Spurs. He is a great player.

Duncan was once a swimmer. He took up basketball as a teenager.

Tim Duncan was born on April 25, 1976. He is from the U.S. Virgin Islands.

Duncan came to the U.S. mainland to play basketball for Wake Forest University.

After college, Duncan joined the Spurs. He played well and was named **Rookie** of the Year.

In 1999, Duncan's great playing helped the Spurs win their very first **championship**.

Duncan was named the NBA's most **valuable** player, or MVP, in both 2002 and 2003.

In 2005 and 2007, Duncan and the Spurs won championships again.

When he is not playing basketball, Duncan does a lot of work for **charity**.

On or off the court,
Tim Duncan is a
great player to look
up to!

BOOKS

Here are more books to read about Tim Duncan and basketball:

Glaser, Jason. *Tim Duncan*. Sports Idols. New York: PowerKids Press, 2008.

Savage, Jeff. *Tim Duncan*. Amazing Athletes. Minneapolis, MN: First Avenue Editions, 2009.

WEB SITES

Due to the changing nature of Internet links, PowerKids Press has developed an online list of Web sites related to the subject of this book. This site is updated regularly. Please use this link to access the list:
www.powerkidslinks.com/bmvp/timdunc/

GLOSSARY

championship (CHAM-pee-un-ship) A group of games played to decide the best, or the winner.

charity (CHER-uh-tee) Helping the needy.

rookie (RU-kee) A new major-league player.

valuable (VAL-yoo-bul) Important.

INDEX